THE LAST OF THE THORNTONS

BY HORTON FOOTE

★

★

DRAMATISTS
PLAY SERVICE
INC.

THE LAST OF THE THORNTONS
Copyright © 2001 (Revised), Horton Foote
Copyright © 1999, Horton Foote

All Rights Reserved

SPECIAL NOTE

Anyone receiving permission to produce THE LAST OF THE THORNTONS is required to give credit to the Author as sole and exclusive Author of the Play on the title page of all programs distributed in connection with performances of the Play and in all instances in which the title of the Play appears for purposes of advertising, publicizing or otherwise exploiting the Play and/or a production thereof. The name of the Author must appear on a separate line, in which no other name appears, immediately beneath the title and in size of type equal to 50% of the size of the largest, most prominent letter used for the title of the Play. No person, firm or entity may receive credit larger or more prominent than that accorded the Author. The following acknowledgment must appear on the title page in all programs distributed in connection with performances of the Play:

World premiere originally produced by
Signature Theatre Company, New York City
James Houghton, Founding Artistic Director
Bruce E. Whitacre, Managing Director

This Play was originally produced with the assistance of the Kennedy Center Fund
for New American Plays, a project of the John F. Kennedy Center
for the Performing Arts with support from the Andrew W. Mellon Foundation
and Countrywide Home Loans, Inc., in cooperation
with the President's Committee on the Arts and Humanities.

SPECIAL NOTE ON SONGS AND RECORDINGS

For performances of copyrighted songs, arrangements or recordings mentioned in this Play, the permission of the copyright owner(s) must be obtained. Other songs, arrangements or recordings may be substituted provided permission from the copyright owner(s) of such songs, arrangements or recordings is obtained; or songs, arrangements or recordings in the public domain may be substituted.

THE LAST OF THE THORNTONS was produced by the Signature Theatre Company (James Houghton, Founding Artistic Director; Bruce E. Whitacre, Managing Director) in New York City on December 3, 2000. It was directed by James Houghton; the set design was by Christine Jones; the lighting design was by Michael Chybowski; the sound design was by Kurt Kellenberger; the costume design was by Elizabeth Hope Clancy; and the production stage manager was Tina M. Newhauser. The cast was as follows:

MISS PEARL DAYTON	Alice McLane
FANNIE MAE GOSSETT	Estelle Parsons
CLARABELLE JONES	Cherene Snow
MRS. RUBY BLAIR	Anne Pitoniak
ORA SUE	Mary Catherine Garrison
ALBERTA THORNTON	Hallie Foote
LEWIS REAVIS	Mason Adams
ANNIE GAYLE LONG	Jen Jones
DOUGLAS JACKSON	Michael Hadge
HARRY VAUGHN, JR.	Timothy Altmeyer

CHARACTERS

FANNIE MAE
MISS PEARL
CLARABELLE
ORA SUE
MRS. RUBY BLAIR *12*
ALBERTA THORNTON
LEWIS REAVIS
ANNIE GAYLE LONG
DOUGLAS JACKSON
HARRY

PLACE

Harrison, Texas.
The front room of a small brick nursing home.

TIME

Spring 1970.

THE LAST OF THE THORNTONS

ACT ONE

Harrison, Texas. Spring 1970.

The front room of a small brick nursing home. The building is of a nondescript architectural style from the 1960s. In the small box-like front room there are brick walls stage right and stage left. Upstage center, a wheelchair ramp has been installed, alongside a small set of stairs, to provide access to a raised upper level upstage of the front room.

The sitting room is neatly arranged with mismatched pieces of furniture, all of which seem past their prime. Fluorescent lighting panels hang overhead illuminating yellowing plaster upstage walls, a cold blue gray tile floor and the faded upholstery and varnish of aged furniture. Despite its aged quality the room appears to be clean and well-kept. The furnishings have been arranged in three areas: a modest reception area stage right, a conversation area center stage, and an isolated armchair downstage left.

Downstage right situated in the brick wall, is the front entrance to the nursing home — a white self-closing door with a metal push-bar and four small windows through which can be seen the tall distressed-looking gray brick wall that surrounds the yard. Above the door is a burnt-out red "exit" sign. Metal conduit runs along the brick. Upstage of the door, a large window faces out to the courtyard (stage right). The window is mostly covered by venetian blinds, which are slanted closed to block out the bright heat of the Texas sun. The blinds are raised only slightly to allow for several potted plants that have been placed along the broad windowsill. Lush green shrubbery and the trunks of small trees can be seen through the slight opening in the blinds.

Downstage right is a modest reception area. Positioned along the stage right brick wall, between the door and window, are a small blue-cloth-covered waiting-room chair, a small side-table where newspapers are kept and a metal umbrella stand with two umbrellas. Just left of the window is the receptionist's small, gray, metal desk crowded with office supplies, a potted plant, framed photographs, a telephone, pencil cup, desk lamp, and candy dish. Behind the desk, positioned in the upstage right corner of the lower level is a four-drawer metal file cabinet on top of which sits potted plants, a box of facial tissues, framed photographs, a water pitcher and paper cups. On the upstage wall hangs a bulletin board crowded with posted memos, photographs and picture postcards. Also on the wall is a metal lock box, a metal rack holding files and an intercom system with a phone receiver.

Stage left of the reception area there is a wheelchair ramp with white metal handrails along its stage right and left sides. The ramp runs upstage to a raised second level. Stage left of the ramp is a narrow set of stairs with four steps.

Center stage, just stage left of the stairs, is a dingy reddish-brown brick half-wall, on the top of which is a planter filled with large-leafed houseplants. Above the half-wall the raised upper level can be seen. In front of the half-wall, on the lower level, is a large dusty brown three-cushion couch. The couch is the principal gathering area for the residents of the home. Its dreary, rough, upholstery is enlivened by a bright multi-colored, knitted afghan that has been draped across its back. Stage left of the couch is a white wooden end table with a few magazines and a dish of hard candies. A floor lamp and a wastebasket are nearby stage left. Downstage left of the couch, an armchair and small folding table complete the conversation area. The armchair is a metal-framed, black vinyl upholstered office chair, the kind that might be seen in the waiting rooms of hospitals or doctors' offices. The folding table is a simple narrow metal stand with a wooden top. On top of the stand, a set of cards is spread out in the formation of an unfinished game of solitaire.

Across the room, situated downstage in the stage left brick wall is a small window completely covered by yellowed venetian blinds. Just upstage of the window, along the same wall, is a twenty-five-gallon aquarium with a lacquered wooden top. The aquarium is brightly illuminated and filled with small shining goldfish. A plastic dolphin decoration is attached to the wall above the aquarium. In the upstage left corner of the lower level, positioned diagonally between the stage left and upstage brick walls is a bright turquoise, vinyl-covered armchair with natural wood-colored arms. Stage right of the chair is a metal magazine stand, displaying three shelves full of magazines — Life, Look, National Geographic, *etc.*

Far downstage left, to the right of the small stage left window, is an isolated armchair with a small circular metal-framed side table. The armchair has warm brown wooden arms. Its spring-cushioned seat is upholstered in faded drab green vinyl. It is the kind of chair that might have once been used in a lawyer's office. The chair faces downstage toward the audience.

Farthest upstage, on the raised upper level, several doors can be seen positioned in yellowing plaster walls. On the down-stage right side of the platform, just upstage of the wheelchair ramp, a thin white door with a brass knob opens into a linen closet. Upstage of this door is the opening to a hallway that leads to the residents' rooms and presumably to another exit as indicated by an exit sign with arrow pointing stage right on the upstage wall. A stainless steel water fountain has been installed in the center of the upstage wall. To the right of the water fountain, an ashtray is also mounted in the wall. To the left of the fountain, near the ceiling panels, is an intercom speaker. Stage left of the water fountain, a plaster wall forms a right angle that encloses Alberta Thornton's room. The entrance to her room is marked by a door facing stage left. Downstage of Alberta's room is a narrow walkway, bordered on its downstage side by the brick half-wall. The walkway leads to the open doorway of the bathroom. The upstage wall of the walkway displays a large painting of a winter landscape. Through the open bathroom doorway stage left, a porcelain washbasin can be seen. Hanging left of the wash-basin, on a wallpapered wall, is a soap dispenser and a rack for hand towels. In the dark, a piano outlines a variation of "The Sheik of Araby." The lights come up. Miss Pearl Dayton, in her early fifties, comes hurrying in, having exited Alberta's room and closing the door behind her. She goes to the phone on her desk and dials.

MISS PEARL. Douglas Jackson, please. Yes, it is pressing. It's kind of an emergency. Yes. No. Nothing personal. It has to do with his cousin, at least my records list him as a cousin of a Miss Alberta Thornton. Yes. Tell him if he could come over as soon as possible. She is misbehaving and refuses to obey the rules and we are very distressed. Thank you. I'll hold. *(Miss Fannie Mae Gossett, a thin, birdlike woman in her late seventies enters carrying two small brown paper bags.)*
FANNIE MAE. Hello, there.
MISS PEARL. I'll be with you in a minute. Have a seat, please.
FANNIE MAE. *(Crosses to the couch.)* I'm Fannie Mae Gossett.
MISS PEARL. Yes, I remember you. I'll be off the phone in a minute. *(Into the phone.)* Yes? Oh. Thank you. Then we can expect him within the hour? Oh, thank you. You are most kind. *(Fannie Mae starts to sit on the couch. When Miss Pearl hangs up, Fannie Mae stands. Miss Pearl crosses toward Fannie Mae.)* Yes, Miss Fannie Mae.
FANNIE MAE. I'm from the drugstore. Gossett's.
MISS PEARL. Yes, I remember.

FANNIE MAE. I've brought medicine for Alberta Thornton and Annie Gayle Long.

MISS PEARL. All right, thank you. Just leave it here with me, and I'll see that they get it.

FANNIE MAE. Thank you, but if you don't mind, I'll take it to them myself and get in a little visit. I've known them both all of my life.

MISS PEARL. Oh?

FANNIE MAE. We all grew up together here. Not that we're the same age. I'm older. I'm a year or two older than Annie, although we would have graduated from high school at the same time, if she had graduated here from high school, but her parents sent her away her junior year and she graduated in a private school up north someplace.

MISS PEARL. *(Crosses stage left and begins cleaning and organizing the room.)* I see.

FANNIE MAE. The reason I was a grade behind what I should have been was that my sweet mother wanted my brother and me to start school at the same time. He is two years younger, so that meant I was older then everybody else in my class.

MISS PEARL. I see.

FANNIE MAE. And I'm a good twenty years older than Alberta Thornton.

MISS PEARL. Uh. Huh.

FANNIE MAE. Alberta Thornton was the cutest little girl.

MISS PEARL. Uh. Huh.

FANNIE MAE. The pet of the town. She was a cheerleader and was voted Miss Personality, or something like that, in her senior year of high school. She was crazy about the movies growing up. Always talking about going off to Hollywood. Whenever she signed her name, she always put H.O.B. after it. I asked her once what that meant and she said Hollywood or Bust. Well, bless her heart, she didn't get to Hollywood, did she?

MISS PEARL. No, bless her heart, she sure didn't.

FANNIE MAE. I think I'll go visit with Alberta Thornton first.

MISS PEARL. I'm sorry. You can't see her now.

FANNIE MAE. No.

MISS PEARL. No.

FANNIE MAE. Is she sleeping?

MISS PEARL. No, she's not sleeping. She's being naughty. She's insisting on sitting in her room naked.

FANNIE MAE. Mercy.

MISS PEARL. We're having to keep a nurse with her in her room to keep her from walking in the halls naked.

FANNIE MAE. Mercy. Mercy. Precious child.

MISS PEARL. We've sent for her cousin, Douglas Jackson.

FANNIE MAE. Oh, yes, his mother raised Alberta Thornton you know.

MISS PEARL. No, I didn't know that.

FANNIE MAE. Oh, yes. Alberta Thornton and Douglas Jackson are first cousins. She and her two sisters were orphaned when she was only eight years old. Then their aunts each took a girl to raise. Miss Loula, the oldest, took the oldest child, Rowena, and Miss Inez, the middle sister, took the middle child, Gloria, and Miss Gert, the youngest sister, Douglas' mother, took Alberta, the youngest child. They were remarkable women these aunts. Each in her own way. Now her aunts are dead and her sisters are dead. Rowena married and divorced. Gloria married twice. She had a child, a boy, as I remember by her second marriage. Alberta never married. They all moved to Houston finally to live together and to raise Gloria's boy. He must be a grown man by now.

MISS PEARL. Yes. He lives in Houston according to what is on her file. He's hard to get hold of, and when we do, he says he can't do anything with her and to do the best we can, and I tell him if she can't mind and walks around naked, we'll have to send her away because we're not equipped to handle something like that. This is really a home for old people, all very genteel. (*Clarabelle, a black woman in her mid-forties, enters from Alberta's room, closing the door behind her. She is large and strong. She goes to the restroom and washes her hands.*)

CLARABELLE. She's putting her clothes on. I told her the moment she starts taking them off again I'll march her back in that room and see she stays there.

MISS PEARL. (*She goes back to her desk and continues organizing.*) Did you tell her if she doesn't behave and keep her clothes on, we won't be able to keep her here any longer and — *(Clarabelle exits the bathroom and stands at the top of the stairs.)*

CLARABELLE. *(Interrupting.)* I can't tell her nothing. She keeps after me all the time to forgive her. Forgive you for what, I ask her? For slavery, she says.

FANNIE MAE. What?

CLARABELLE. *(Going down the stairs.)* For slavery. I said to her, you are talking to the wrong woman. I never been nobody's slave.

FANNIE MAE. I think I'll go and see Annie Gayle Long first.

CLARABELLE. You can't see her for another half-hour. She's being given a bath.

FANNIE MAE. That's all right. I'll wait. I was here to see her last week you know.

CLARABELLE. Did she talk to you?

FANNIE MAE. No.

CLARABELLE. *(She crosses to stage right chair near the door and sits.)* And she ain't gonna talk to you. She won't talk to nobody. I don't know why they brought her back here.

FANNIE MAE. *(At the foot of the stairs.)* She's got people here. Distant cousins mostly, but they are kin.

CLARABELLE. They don't never come to see her. Do they?

MISS PEARL. No.

FANNIE MAE. Well, everybody is so busy these days, and most of her friends are dead or moved away. *(Fannie Mae sits on the couch.)* I hardly know anyone here anymore myself, and I've lived here all my life. *(Pause. Miss Pearl attends to work at her desk. Fannie Mae looks around the room.)* I remember when this was a sweet little two-room hospital. It was the old Philips house and the doctors bought it and turned it into a hospital. *(Miss Pearl leans against her desk as she listens.)* It was a two-story frame house, you know. The waiting room was the parlor, and the operating room was the dining room, and upstairs was the rooms for the patients, and I think there was a room down here for patients, too. Half the town, you know, was born here.

CLARABELLE. Were you born here?

FANNIE MAE. No. I was born at home. It wasn't until the early twenties we started having our babies in hospitals.

MISS PEARL. Were your babies born here?

FANNIE MAE. I have no babies, lady. I've never married.

MISS PEARL. Is that so?

FANNIE MAE. Sad things happened here, too. Dr. Leo's wife Louise died here. In childbirth. He saved many lives, and he couldn't save his own wife's life. The whole town was grieved so.

MISS PEARL. What happened to the two-story frame house?

FANNIE MAE. They tore it down. It had a gallery upstairs and down. It was on that front gallery that Dr. White said he heard this thud. Dr. White was Dr. Leo's father. Galbraith was their last name. And he said it was still dark and he had come here to see a patient and he heard this thud on the front gallery and he thought it was a farmer leaving a sack of potatoes in payment for a bill. And then he said he heard a moan and he went out there and there was Jimmie Dale bleeding to death lying on the porch where he had been thrown.

CLARABELLE. God Almighty. Who had thrown him?

FANNIE MAE. A cousin, Roger Higgens. They had dated these two women, a redheaded woman named Mrs. Goodwin and a black-haired woman I forget her name that Mrs. Goodwin introduced around town as her companion. They lived out in the country someplace and Jimmie Dale and Roger Higgens had dates with them that night and they all got to drinking and then fighting and Roger Higgens took out a knife and cut Jimmie Dale. *(She uses her throat to demonstrate.)* From here to here. And they came by the hospital and threw his body on the gallery.

CLARABELLE. Merciful God. Uh. Did you ever hear that before?

MISS PEARL. No.

CLARABELLE. Merciful God. When did all this happen?

FANNIE MAE. A long time ago. 1925 as well as I can remember. In the fall. And Jimmie Dale was so handsome. Twenty-one years old. He didn't last but a day. Half the town was out in the yard there and in the street, praying he wouldn't die, but die he did. His poor mother screaming and cursing like a lunatic. "Give me back my boy, give me back my boy, give me back my boy!"

MISS PEARL. *(Moves downstage.)* What happened to the one that killed him?

FANNIE MAE. There was a trial. It tore the town apart. As I said they were kin to each other so it was cousin against cousin. Roger

Higgen's people got the best lawyer they could find, cost them I don't know what all.

MISS PEARL. What happened?

FANNIE MAE. Roger Higgens got off. He's dead now, too. I think he was kin to Alberta Thornton. *(Mrs. Ruby Blair, 72, is wheeled in by a young girl, Ora Sue, 18, from upstage left in the home.)*

MISS PEARL. Going for a ride? *(Clarabelle goes upstage and takes over wheeling Mrs. Blair down the ramp.)*

MRS. RUBY BLAIR. I'm going to my daughter's and spend the day.

MISS PEARL. That's lovely. Have a nice time.

MRS. RUBY BLAIR. *(As she is wheeled down the ramp.)* Thank you. This is my granddaughter, Ora Sue.

MISS PEARL. Hello, Ora Sue.

ORA SUE. *(Taking over the wheelchair at the front of the ramp.)* Hello.

MRS. RUBY BLAIR. She's just been elected cheerleader at the high school.

MISS PEARL. Well congratulations, Ora Sue.

ORA SUE. Thank you.

MISS PEARL. Have a nice time. *(They continue on as her granddaughter wheels her out the door which Miss Pearl holds open.)*

FANNIE MAE. I don't think I know her. Is she from around here?

MISS PEARL. *(At her desk.)* No. From out in the country. Blossom Prairie way. Her husband was a rice farmer.

FANNIE MAE. Uh huh. Where is her husband?

MISS PEARL. Dead.

CLARABELLE. *(Standing in front of Miss Pearl's desk.)* Died right here.

FANNIE MAE. Where?

CLARABELLE. Right here in this office. He came out to ask us something and he fell over dead.

FANNIE MAE. Bless his heart. *(To Miss Pearl.)* Were you here, honey?

MISS PEARL. No. I was off that day. Thank God.

CLARABELLE. Poor old thing. He was talking as good as you. Just as pleasant, and, my God, right in front of my eyes, he just fell over. I screamed and hollered. Said they thought I was being

13

killed. Wouldn't you know it, there wasn't a doctor on the place. Somebody ran for his poor wife and brought her out in the wheelchair and I had got control by then and was feeling his pulse and trying to talk to him, and this other nurse came in then and said, Clarabelle, no use talking to him, he's dead. How do you know, I said. Cause I know, she said. And she went over to him and leaned down and listened to his heartbeat, and said again, dead. And his poor wife was crying by then and her friend that wheeled her in was trying to comfort her and it was a mess. *(Alberta Thornton, 60, comes out of her room dressed in a simple but becoming dress. Clarabelle retreats to her chair stage right.)*

MISS PEARL. Why Miss Alberta, what a pretty dress. *(Alberta goes to the top of the stairs and stops, looking at Clarabelle.)*

ALBERTA. I ask for your forgiveness. *(She crosses down right in front of Clarabelle.)*

CLARABELLE. Now, Lord have mercy, don't start that, lady.

ALBERTA. I can't rest until you forgive me.

MISS PEARL. Tell her you forgive her, Clarabelle.

CLARABELLE. I got nothing to forgive her for. I'm nobody's slave. I'm free as she is. Shoot. *(Clarabelle exits upstage and sits in the chair just downstage of Alberta's room. Alberta cries.)*

ALBERTA. I feel so guilty.

FANNIE MAE. *(Stands.)* Honey, what's wrong?

ALBERTA. I feel so guilty. I'm being punished.

FANNIE MAE. For what, honey?

ALBERTA. *(Crosses to Fannie Mae in front of the couch.)* For slavery.

FANNIE MAE. Mercy, you didn't have anything to do with slavery. That was before your time, darling.

ALBERTA. She was a slave on our plantation.

FANNIE MAE. No, she wasn't, darling. She wasn't ever a slave on anybody's plantation. You never had a plantation, honey. You were born here in town. Your great-grandfather had a plantation.

ALBERTA. And a hundred and seventy slaves.

FANNIE MAE. I don't know about that.

ALBERTA. *(To Miss Pearl and Fannie Mae.)* A hundred and seventy slaves that he brought here from Alabama. I was living in West University in Houston, you know with my sisters and when they died ... Gloria died first, you know, and then Rowena and I

14

was alone in that house in West University in Houston and late one night I heard this commotion and people trying to get into my house and I knew it was my great-grandfather's slaves trying to get to me, to kill me, but I looked out the window and I saw it wasn't slaves, but hippies, and they were going to come and kill me and I called my cousin Edgar and he said, Alberta, take another tranquilizer and go back to sleep and that's what I did.

FANNIE MAE. You see. There weren't any slaves. Slavery is all over. Alberta, how were you kin to Roger Higgens?

ALBERTA. He killed Jimmie Dale. Did you all know Jimmie Dale?

FANNIE MAE. No, they didn't know him, darling. They're newcomers. I was just telling them about him.

ALBERTA. Jimmie Dale was very handsome.

FANNIE MAE. Indeed he was.

ALBERTA. *(Pointing out the door.)* They left his body right out on that porch.

FANNIE MAE. Not on that porch, sweetheart. There was a frame house here then, remember? It was one of our lovely old southern homes that they turned into a hospital. Were you and Roger Higgens second or third cousins?

ALBERTA. Second cousins once removed.

FANNIE MAE. *(Sits.)* That's how it was.

ALBERTA. *(Sits next to Fannie Mae on the couch.)* I was the first white child born in Harrison.

FANNIE MAE. No, you weren't, honey. That was Mrs. Gallahow. And she's been dead fifty years. You probably don't remember her, darling. But I do. She drove a buggy to town every day.

ALBERTA. I'm going home. *(Alberta gets up and crosses to the door. Clarabelle races down and, along with Miss Pearl, blocks her exit. Fannie Mae stands.)*

CLARABELLE. You're not going no place except back to your room.

ALBERTA. I'm going home.

CLARABELLE. How? You got no home here no more. *(Alberta crosses to stage left window.)* Your home is in Houston, and that's fifty-five miles away. How you going to get there? Walk?

ALBERTA. *(Partly to Fannie Mae as she passes her.)* I'm going home.

CLARABELLE. Call her cousin. Tell him to get over here.

(Alberta looks through the slats of the stage left window.)
MISS PEARL. I called him, I told you. He said he'd be right over.
CLARABELLE. *(Exiting up the ramp.)* He's got to start making
her behave or take her someplace else. She's wearing me out.
MISS PEARL. Let's all keep calm.
CLARABELLE. *(Coming back to ramp.)* She's wearing me out.
Either she starts behaving sensibly or she leaves or I leave. Shoot.
(She leaves. A pause. Alberta looks over at Fannie Mae.)
ALBERTA. I wonder where all those slaves are now? *(Alberta sits
in the stage left chair.)*
FANNIE MAE. They must be all dead, darling. *(Lewis Reavis, 85,
still active and alert, comes in.)* Hello, Lewis. Fannie Mae Gossett.
Remember me?
LEWIS. I remember you. *(He crosses to stage right table near
Clarabelle's chair and takes the newspaper.)* I've got no home
anymore, you know. They tore my house down.
FANNIE MAE. I don't think it was your house, Lewis. I think
you rented it. How's Edith?
LEWIS. Edith is dead.
FANNIE MAE. *(To Miss Pearl.)* Edith was his sister.
LEWIS. Edith is dead.
FANNIE MAE. I know. I heard you, Lewis. I'm so sorry to hear
that.
LEWIS. *(He crosses to his chair center stage.)* Thank you.
FANNIE MAE. When did she die?
LEWIS. Two months ago next Sunday. Her obituary was in the
paper.
FANNIE MAE. I'm sorry I didn't see it.
LEWIS. Her husband is dead too.
FANNIE MAE. *(Sitting on couch.)* What was his name?
LEWIS. *(Sitting.)* Mr. Lack. Edith said he was well named. She
said next time she was going to marry someone named
Abundance. My mama is dead.
FANNIE MAE. Oh, yes, I knew that. Where was Edith living
when she died?
LEWIS. Gulf Port. Lucille is dead.
FANNIE MAE. Yes, I knew that too. *(To Miss Pearl.)* Lucille was
his wife.

LEWIS. She and my mama didn't get along and she divorced me and she died. She couldn't make her children mind.

FANNIE MAE. They weren't your children were they, Lewis?

LEWIS. Hell no. They were Billy Ferguson's. He died in the flu epidemic of 1918. Lucille was a widow when I married her.

FANNIE MAE. I remember. That was a terrible time for us all. The flu. Did you get the flu?

LEWIS. No. I tried to get in the army though, but they wouldn't take me. They said I was too nervous and I had flat feet and curvature of the spine. Your brother went to the army didn't he?

FANNIE MAE. Yes, he did.

LEWIS. Was that the First World War or the Second?

FANNIE MAE. Gracious, Lewis. The First.

LEWIS. I get my wars all mixed up these days. His name is Foxhurst, isn't it?

FANNIE MAE. Yes.

LEWIS. And you call him Bubba?

FANNIE MAE. Yes.

LEWIS. And he calls you Sister?

FANNIE MAE. He certainly does.

LEWIS. *(Gets up and goes to the couch.)* The Whitten boy got gassed in the First World War. Did Bubba get gassed?

FANNIE MAE. No. Came home without a scratch. *(Lewis sits on the couch. Fannie Mae moves away one space on the couch. Miss Pearl continues with work at her desk. Alberta remains seated.)*

LEWIS. When Lucille and I got married I said we were going to have to live with Mama, and she said all right but I'll have to have my children with me, all except Frances Jane because she wants to live with her dead daddy's people, and I asked Mama and she said all right and so we got married and moved in, but Lucille couldn't ever say no to her children and she wouldn't let anybody else lay a hand on them, and the children and their noise were driving Mama crazy, and I said, Lucille my Mama comes first with me, always has and always will. Well, I can take a hint, she said, I'll take my children and go and she did and she went back to her mama and papa, and I met her uptown one day after we got divorced and I asked her how she was doing and she said not well at all. And I asked what was the matter and she said her papa was worse than my mama. He complained all the time about her children and besides it was so crowded she could hardly stand it. And when I told Mama that, she said, no wonder it's crowded, she's got her brothers Sonny and Donald and Leroy and her sisters Katie and Louise and Mary and Josephine, and sometimes her brother and sister that are married come for the weekend with their children, all living at once in that house. Well, it's a big house, Mama, I said. Not big enough for that crowd. She just looked pitiful, Mama, I said, and Mama said, I don't care how pitiful she looks, don't you ever think about marrying and bringing her and those children back here.

FANNIE MAE. She got married again, didn't she?

LEWIS. Yes.

FANNIE MAE. Married a man from Flatonia?

LEWIS. Yes. And moved there. I never saw her again but once and she'd gotten as fat as her mama. Do you remember how fat her mama was? Lucille died before Mama did. I said, Mama maybe we ought to send flowers, but Mama said, no she didn't think it would be proper and Mr. Casey ...

FANNIE MAE. (Interrupting.) Who's Mr. Casey?

LEWIS. The man from Flatonia that she married. I heard he said he couldn't make those children behave either.

FANNIE MAE. What was the name of the children? I forgot.

LEWIS. Frances Jane, she was the oldest, then Sister and Billy, named for his daddy, Mr. Ferguson. Frances Jane had a rotten disposition. The day Lucille brought me over to the house and said, Frances Jane this is gonna be your new daddy, she spit at me.

FANNIE MAE. Mercy! What did Lucille say to her?

LEWIS. Nothing. She just turned to me and said, don't pay her any mind, she's just high strung. (A pause as Fannie Mae glances over at Alberta.)

FANNIE MAE. Lewis, you remember Alberta Thornton?

LEWIS. Yes, Ma'am. Is she dead? I haven't seen her in I don't know when.

FANNIE MAE. She's not dead, Lewis.

LEWIS. Most people I know are.

FANNIE MAE. Well, she's not, honey. (She points to Alberta.) Who's that there?

LEWIS. Where?

FANNIE MAE. Right where I'm pointing.

LEWIS. I don't know.

FANNIE MAE. That's Alberta Thornton.

LEWIS. *(He starts to walk over to Alberta.)* Go on. My God, she's changed.

FANNIE MAE. We've all changed, Lewis.

LEWIS. *(Standing stage right of Alberta.)* Hello, Alberta. Forgive me for not recognizing you. I remember you as a girl. You were a pretty little thing. I'm Lewis Reavis. Didn't you work at one time for the gas company? *(Alberta doesn't answer.)*

FANNIE MAE. Honey, did you work for the gas company? *(A pause.)* If memory serves me, I think you did.

LEWIS. *(Crossing back between Fannie Mae and Alberta.)* I know she did. I used to come to her to pay my bill every month. I always paid in cash. Once they turned my gas off by mistake and I came in to report it and Alberta was gone. There was a new girl working there then, what was her name? Sibyl? Louise? I can't remember, but I said, where is Alberta? Gone, they said. Gone, where? Left town? No. Just got tired of working. *(He crosses down to Alberta.)* Well, that's a good attitude if you can afford it. I never could. Where you been all these years, Alberta?

ALBERTA. Houston. *(Alberta gets up and starts out.)*

MISS PEARL. Where are you going honey? Back to your room? *(Pause.)* Miss Alberta. *(Alberta doesn't answer and continues on into her room. Miss Pearl picks up the intercom. She speaks into the intercom.)* Clarabelle, Miss Alberta has gone back to her room. Keep an eye on her.

LEWIS. *(Crossing to center stage.)* Her daddy owned the pool hall. I used to play pool there. Albert. Albert Thornton, that was his name. One day I was playing pool there and this man came up to me and said — *(Clarabelle enters from upstage right and sits in the chair near Alberta's door.)* — where's the owner, and I said there he is, pointing to Mr. Albert, and he said, no, that can't be him, he's too aristocratic looking to be running a pool hall. I said, well, that may be, but it is him. He was aristocratic looking, you know. *(Lewis sits on the couch near Fannie Mae.)*

FANNIE MAE. Yes, he was. His grandfather was acting governor during the Mexican war.

LEWIS. That's right. I heard that. Didn't Alberta have two sisters?

FANNIE MAE. Yes. Rowena and Gloria.

LEWIS. Which one's husband committed suicide on their honeymoon?

FANNIE MAE. Gloria's.

LEWIS. I wonder why he did that?

FANNIE MAE. No one ever knew.

LEWIS. Rowena ever marry?

FANNIE MAE. Yes, married and divorced. Gloria married again. Married one of the Vaughn boys.

LEWIS. Which one?

FANNIE MAE. Harry.

LEWIS. My God. They were terrors, weren't they? Had such a fine father too. Where are her sisters now?

FANNIE MAE. Dead.

LEWIS. Whatever happened to the Vaughn boys?

FANNIE MAE. They're all dead.

LEWIS. Well, I'm not surprised. Almost everybody I know is dead. My mama, Edith, my baby brother. Of course he died when he was ten. Lockjaw. Stepped on a rusty nail. Almost killed Mama. *(Alberta returns from her room. Lewis stands. A silence. They watch her cross to her chair downstage left.)* How old are you, Miss Alberta?

ALBERTA. *(Sitting stage left in her chair.)* I don't remember.

FANNIE MAE. She's sixty if she's a day.

LEWIS. Good God Almighty. Sixty. How old are you, Miss Fannie Mae?

FANNIE MAE. Seventy-eight *(Clarabelle exits.)*

LEWIS. *(Crosses to his chair.)* I'm eighty-five. Mama was ninety when she died. I pray to God I don't outlive you, Lewis, she said. Well, she didn't. She got her wish. *(Lewis sits. There is thunder.)*

ALBERTA. Hear the thunder? I bet it's going to rain. *(Fannie Mae heads toward stage right window. There is thunder again.)* I hope it rains and rains and rains. *(The intercom buzzer rings, Miss Pearl picks up the intercom phone.)*

MISS PEARL. Yes, I'll tell her. *(She hangs up the phone. To Fannie Mae.)* Miss Annie has had her bath now, if you want to go see her. *(A beat. They listen to the rain coming down now in torrents.)*

FANNIE MAE. Thank you. *(Crossing back to center stage.)* Alberta, I'm going to visit Annie Gayle Long now in her room. Do you remember her?

ALBERTA. No.

FANNIE MAE. She's been away for a very long time. What year were you born, Alberta?

ALBERTA. I don't remember.

MISS PEARL. It says here on your record, Miss Alberta. You were born in 1910.

LEWIS. Where has Annie Gayle Long been all this time?

FANNIE MAE. *(Moving closer to Lewis.)* Well, she went off to school in the North someplace and then she married and lived in Houston and after the birth of her two children she began to have nervous troubles and they sent her away to an — *(Spelling as she moves closer yet.)* — A-S-Y-L-U-M. But when you see her don't mention that because she might be sensitive about it. *(To Alberta.)* Want to go with me, honey, to visit her? I think she gets lonely.

ALBERTA. No, thank you. *(Again there is thunder.)*

FANNIE MAE. I have some medicine for you your doctor ordered. Shall I give it to you or take it to your room?

MISS PEARL. *(Crossing to the stairs to meet Fannie Mae.)* Give it to me. I'll have the nurse take it to her room. Thank you. *(Fannie Mae gives her the medicine and leaves upstage right.)*

ALBERTA. *(A pause. To Lewis.)* Do you remember Jimmie Dale?

LEWIS. *(Turning toward her in his chair.)* He's dead. Roger Higgens killed him. He said he wasn't a southern gentlemen because he didn't respect women and so he killed him.

ALBERTA. Roger Higgens was my second cousin once removed.

LEWIS. Second cousin once removed. Is that how it was? I knew you were kin some way. He could have been a rich man, you know. He and his brother inherited a fine plantation.

ALBERTA. They stole it. Their granddaddy stole it from my granddaddy when he was eighteen.

LEWIS. How did he do that?

ALBERTA. I don't know but they did. Some way. A long time ago. It was all explained to me once, but I don't remember now. Didn't do them any good. None of it's left. Sold off piece by piece. Anyway that's always happening to the Thorntons. The Thorntons

21

steal from each other. You remember my sister, Gloria, who married Henry Vaughn? *(Alberta gets up and crosses to the couch.)*

LEWIS. Yes. A pretty woman.

ALBERTA. Well, they had a son named Little Harry. *(She sits on the couch.)* And when his grandmother died she left him a farm and sixty thousand dollars. His mother begged him and Rowena begged him and I begged him to put the money away for a rainy day. But he wouldn't listen. Spent it on I don't know what all. As soon as he could.

LEWIS. I remember hearing about that boy. When they were casting some picture and they wanted a southern boy and — *(Alberta imagines she hears something at the front entrance to the room and hurries across the room to the front door. Miss Pearl hurries from behind her desk to block Alberta's path.)* — they came to Houston looking for one and spotted what was his name?

ALBERTA. Little Harry.

LEWIS. That's right. I read all about it in the *Houston Chronicle.* What was the name of the picture? *(Alberta thinking now she hears something outside the stage left window hurries across the room to the window.)*

ALBERTA. *(As she crosses.)* The Yearling.

LEWIS. And they took him to Hollywood to screen test him. Did he get the part?

ALBERTA. *(Peeking out the window.)* No.

LEWIS. That was a shame. Did you go out there with him?

ALBERTA. We all did. His mother, Rowena, and myself. We sure did.

LEWIS. How did you like Hollywood? *(Alberta crosses upstage now checking the hall and closing the door to her room, the linen closet and the restroom.)*

ALBERTA. To tell you the truth I was disappointed.

LEWIS. Is that so? I know I'd be. Everybody is always going on about California this and California that. I like Texas and I don't want to go any place else. Not California, not New York City. I was born where it's flat and I hope to die where it's flat. *(A pause.)* Where is what's his name now?

ALBERTA. Little Harry?

LEWIS. Yes.

ALBERTA. He's in Houston trying to get hold of my property.

LEWIS. You have property in Houston?

ALBERTA. *(At the top of the stairs.)* Yes. A duplex in West University which has become a very exclusive part of town.

LEWIS. Why is he trying to take your property?

ALBERTA. Because he drinks and he needs money all the time. He went through the sixty thousand his grandmother left him and then he mortgaged the farm and he lost that to our cousin.

LEWIS. Which cousin?

ALBERTA. Douglas Jackson.

LEWIS. Oh yes.

ALBERTA. Now I'm nervous, you see, and I can't stay alone anymore and Little Harry brought me here to have someone look out for me, and he says he can't afford to keep me here and I have to let him sell the duplex and I tell him no way in this world, because he'll spend it all on drink and fast living and then there'll be nothing. I had renters on the top floor, but Little Harry says they're gone now and if I don't sell the duplex it will be taken for taxes, but I don't believe him. And he's gone to our cousin Douglas Jackson, who's a lawyer, to handle the transaction, he says, if I agree to sell the duplex and in the meantime Douglas Jackson would advance us some money to pay my bills here, and I said, you know what will happen if you get him involved? *(Crosses to the front of the couch.)* He'll end up with the whole thing, just like he did your farm when you mortgaged that to him. Anyway, I'm going to go back to Houston after I rest a little bit more. I think I'm over being nervous. You see I kept thinking these blacks were coming after me, but then I looked out this window and they weren't blacks, they were hippies.

LEWIS. Hippies?

ALBERTA. Yessir. Hippies as far as my eyes could see. But I called my cousin Edgar out in California and he said, take a tranquilizer and go on back to sleep, and I did, but I didn't want to stay alone after that, but I think now I'm calmer and I can make out. I get a little government check and once I'm there I can rent the apartment above me.

MISS PEARL. *(Crossing to the ramp.)* Miss Alberta.

ALBERTA. Yes.

MISS PEARL. Your cousin Douglas Jackson is coming over here.

ALBERTA. I don't want my cousin Douglas Jackson over here. *(Crossing to Miss Pearl.)* He steals everything in sight. Land. Houses. Farms. He's the one who got Little Harry's farm. Is it still raining?

MISS PEARL. Slightly now.

ALBERTA. *(Crosses and sits on couch.)* I'll wait until the rain's over, then I'll go home. *(She sings a song of the period, such as "I Get the Blues When It Rains."* A pause. She looks over at Miss Pearl seated again at her desk.)* Miss Pearl?

MISS PEARL. Yes, Miss Alberta?

ALBERTA. Did your family own slaves?

MISS PEARL. No. Not that I know of.

ALBERTA. Then you're blessed. *(Crosses to stage left window and peers through the slats.)* There was a curse on my family for owning slaves. A curse. *(She turns to Lewis.)* We sold our house here you know.

LEWIS. I remember that house. It was over on Caney Street.

ALBERTA. *(Goes to stage left chair and stands behind it.)* I sometimes think that was a mistake, but my sisters got discouraged and said nothing was going to happen here now and we'd better get on to Houston. My daddy was dead then, but he called me to his bedside just before he died and said, Alberta, do you realize when I die you'll be the last of the Thorntons? And I said, Daddy, that's not right. Gloria and Rowena are Thorntons and our cousin Douglas Jackson, crooked as he is, is a Thornton. But his name isn't Thornton, Daddy said, and Gloria and Rowena married so they don't have the family name, but I have the name, you have the name. Of course, if you marry after I die there will be no one left with the name of Thornton. Promise me you'll never marry.

LEWIS. Did you ever marry?

ALBERTA. No.

LEWIS. I married. It didn't last but a few months but I married. Did you know my sister Edith?

ALBERTA. *(She crosses and goes up the stairs toward her room.)* No.

LEWIS. She died two months ago next Sunday. The obituary was

* See Special Note on Songs and Recordings on copyright page.

24

in the paper. Do you subscribe to the Harrison paper?

ALBERTA. No.

LEWIS. I don't either anymore. It comes out once a week.

ALBERTA. *(Comes back to the top of the stairs and shares her story with Lewis and Miss Pearl.)* I saw a book once that some Yankee lady moved to Houston had and she said are you from Harrison? Yes, ma'am, I said, born and raised there. Did you know a Colonel Thornton? Well, I never knew him, I said, but he was my great-grandfather, why do you ask? Look here, she said, and showed me this book, and it was filled with letters written by women slaves, and there were two letters written by a slave on Colonel Thornton's plantation named Elizabeth Ramsey, and she was writing to her daughter who was freed and living in Ohio. Her daughter wanted to buy her mother and her brother from Colonel Thornton and Elizabeth Ramsey was writing to tell her that Colonel Thornton wouldn't sell her unless her daughter could pay him a thousand dollars for her and fifteen hundred dollars for her brother. *(Alberta stands in front of couch.)*

LEWIS. Fifteen hundred dollars?

ALBERTA. Yes. Then there was a letter written a year later from Elizabeth Ramsey to her daughter and she said Colonel Thornton would take eight hundred dollars for her now, but he wouldn't sell her son for any price because he was training him to be an overseer on his plantation. *(She gasps in terror.)* Shhh … *(She listens.)* Excuse me. *(She moves to look out the window stage left, peeking out.)* I guess I was wrong. I thought I heard people hollering and cursing out there like they were in Houston.

LEWIS. What happened to the slave that wrote the letter? Did her daughter buy her?

ALBERTA. *(Standing upstage of stage left chair.)* I don't know what happened. Sometimes I think she did and sometimes I think she couldn't raise the money. If she bought her, how would she get her from here to Ohio during slavery time? *(A pause.)* No, to tell you the truth Hollywood was a real disappointment. When I came home I threw away all the movie star pictures I had saved all through the years. Richard Dix, Lillian Gish, John Gilbert, Antonio Moreno, the whole lot of them, except Rudolph Valentino and Barbara La Marr, because when they died I vowed to myself I would never forget them, I would always keep their pictures and remember them. I still have them, too, somewhere in my house in Houston, in a drawer somewhere with my mama's pictures and my sisters who are all dead now. I was born in 1910. I remember now.

LEWIS. I expect that's right. That's what Miss Pearl says your record shows. *(Thunder.)*

ALBERTA. My mama died eight years after I was born in 1918. They say it was the flu that killed her, but Rowena doesn't believe that and I don't either. We think she died of a broken heart. *(Again there is thunder.)* Hear that thunder? It thundered the night my mama died. The thunder woke me up and my Aunt Gert was standing by my bed and she said, your mama's dead, honey. You're going to live with me now. My daddy gambled and that broke my mama's heart they say. I had two sisters, Gloria, named for my mama, and Rowena. I forgot who Rowena was named for, some cousin or other. I was named for my father, Albert, and my aunt. Patience Texas Louisiana Thornton who everybody called Loula and she was named for her aunt Patience Texas Louisiana Thornton. My aunt never owned slaves but my great aunt did. Colonel Thornton in his will left half of his slaves to my great aunt and half to my grandfather, but the war came and the slaves were freed. *(She begins to sing a song of the period, such as "I Get the Blues When It Rains."* Alberta goes around Lewis to near the stairs. She laughs.)* I never cared much for school.

LEWIS. Oh, well, neither did I. I wouldn't worry about it.

ALBERTA. *(Sharing her story between Lewis sitting in the chair and Miss Pearl still at her desk. She paces a few steps back and forth between them throughout her speech.)* My aunt worried about that and she used to say, Alberta, take a commercial course, learn typing and shorthand, because you're going to have to take care of yourself, honey. All I have is the farm and with cotton the price it is I just barely am able to put food on the table, and every nickel your daddy earns he gambles away, as you well know. And I listened to her, but my heart wasn't in it. Every day in school I slipped movie magazines into my desk and when the teacher wasn't looking I'd look at the pictures of the movie stars, and I'd

* See Special Note on Songs and Recordings on copyright page.

say to myself Hollywood's where I'm going and nothing is going to stop me. I saw an ad in the *Houston Chronicle* about a man from Hollywood looking for talent and he was giving screen tests and I got Rowena to go with me and I looked up this man and I said, I would like a screen test, and he said, what's your experience? and I said, what do you mean? And he said, have you ever acted? And I said, no, and he said, you'll have to have some acting experience before I can give you a screen test, and I said, how do I go about getting that? And he said, well, I have classes in tap dancing and speech and tips on how to act before the camera, and then he said to me, has anyone ever told you you look like Bebe Daniels? And Rowena said, many people say that and I call her Bebe half the time myself. And then Rowena said, how much do you charge for your lessons? And he said, a hundred dollars for three months, lessons twice a week, morning or evening, take your choice. I start off with the tap dancing, so you'll have to get tap shoes. When do you teach screen acting? I asked. That comes after the tap dancing, the third week. I really don't care about tap dancing, I said. Well, he said, one thing feeds the other, Bebe Daniels can sing and tap dance too. Greta Garbo doesn't tap dance, I said, that's true, he said, but she's Swedish. Well, we'll think about it, Rowena said, and we left. When we got outside Rowena said, that man's a fake.

LEWIS. Was he?

ALBERTA. I guess he was because we read later in the *Houston Chronicle* that he got arrested for taking people's money under false pretenses.

LEWIS. What do you know.

ALBERTA. *(Crosses to stage left.)* Anyway, I never got to Hollywood until we all went out with Little Harry for his screen test, and Rowena said, well, Bebe, here you are at last in Hollywood. *(A pause. Stands behind stage left chair and sometimes she looks to Miss Pearl and Lewis.)* Gloria was the first to get sick. Rowena nursed her night and day, wouldn't let anyone else come near her, not even me. Rowena was the one that kept us all together. The Thornton girls, she used to say, have to stay together. My sister Gloria was a beauty, you know. Everyone said she should be a movie star, but that never interested her. She had two husbands and lots of beaux. Anyway, beauty or not she got sick and Rowena nursed her and she died and we brought her back home here to Harrison to bury her, and Rowena insisted on having a colored picture of her placed on her tombstone, so the world could always see how beautiful she was. *(Alberta goes behind Lewis' chair and lightly touches his shoulder.)* Did you ever see her picture on her tombstone at the cemetery?

LEWIS. No, I sure haven't.

ALBERTA. You ought to go see it some time. It's just beautiful. You ought to go too, Miss Pearl.

MISS PEARL. Thank you. I will one day.

ALBERTA. *(Goes to behind stage left chair and speaks to both of them.)* Anyway, then Rowena got sick, worn out from nursing Gloria I think, and she died and I was alone in that duplex in Houston, which Rowena said was to be mine as long as I lived. Then Little Harry called me and said he thought even though his mother hadn't left a will, her share of the duplex should now be his, but if I wanted to buy him out he would sell me his share for five thousand dollars. Not for five hundred I told him, because all he would do would be to spend it on whiskey and fast living, and then one day he came around with this colored fellow and his name was Ramsey — *(Alberta, suddenly very agitated, crosses toward downstage right door, the exit to the home. Miss Pearl beats her to the door and blocks her path.)* — and his great-granddaddy had been a slave on our great-grandfather's plantation. *(Alberta goes to center stage in front of couch.)*

LEWIS. Is that so?

ALBERTA. Yes.

LEWIS. His name was what?

ALBERTA. Ramsey.

LEWIS. Ramsey. Was he kin to that lady slave whose daughter tried to buy?

ALBERTA. Yes. And I told him about the letters I read in the slave letters book and about the two from Elizabeth Ramsey and he said that was his great-grandfather's mother and she had gotten to Ohio. And that his great-grandfather had stayed on the plantation until the slaves were freed. And he knew from Little Harry of all our troubles and he said that was our family's punishment for owning slaves and the Thornton name was going

28

to vanish from the earth as one punishment and I said, well, why hadn't I died instead of my sisters? I was the last with the Thornton name, I'm still alive. And he said, your punishment's bound to come unless you ask forgiveness. Of whom? I said. Of every colored person you meet from now on beginning with me. And when he left I told Little Harry what he said I should do and Little Harry said I was making the whole thing up, that he's never said anything like that to him and he wasn't responsible for slavery and wasn't going to ask anybody's forgiveness for anything and then that night when I was all alone in the duplex I heard these negroes from my great-grandfather's plantation hollering and screaming outside the duplex, and I went to the window to ask their forgiveness and when I got there, those weren't any blacks at all, but just white hippies, and that's when I called my cousin Edgar out in California and he told me to take a tranquilizer and I did. Anyway, I don't care what Little Harry says, I know what Ramsey said to me, and every time I see a colored person I ask them for forgiveness, and sometimes they grant it and sometimes they don't, but I always feel better for asking. *(Alberta sits. Fannie Mae comes out arm in arm with Annie Gayle Long.)*

FANNIE MAE. Look who's here, Alberta? *(Lewis crosses to stage right near Miss Pearl. Alberta stands.)* She wanted to come out and visit for a while. I think she gets lonely in her room.

MISS PEARL. I'm sure. Hello Miss Annie Gayle.

LEWIS. Hello, Miss Annie.

FANNIE MAE. *(Fannie Mae seats Annie on the couch.)* Here's Annie. Now do you remember her?

ALBERTA. No. I don't.

FANNIE MAE. She remembers you. Don't you, Annie? *(Annie is silent. Fannie Mae leans over to whisper to Alberta.)* Her father had the bank and was killed by Mr. Sledge. I suppose that was all before your time, Alberta, but surely you heard about it.

ALBERTA. Did he have slaves? *(Miss Pearl sits at her desk.)*

FANNIE MAE. No, darling. Her people were from the North. They came here after the war. *(Alberta sits in chair stage left.)*

LEWIS. Which war was that, Miss Fannie Mae? *(He hand signals Fannie Mae to come over to him.)* The war between the states?

FANNIE MAE. No, Lewis. It was the Spanish-American War.

(Fannie Mae crosses to Lewis.)

LEWIS. Oh, I see. *(Whispers to Fannie Mae.)* Mama was uptown the day Mr. Sledge killed Miss Annie's daddy, she said if she had come out of Mr. Alpards' grocery store just a few minutes sooner she would have been witness to the whole thing. Last time Mama told me about Mr. Sledge killing her daddy I said, Mama, what did he kill him for? I don't know exactly, she said. Something about money I never did get it straight.

FANNIE MAE. *(Whispering.)* I remember very well what it was about. I went to the trial, the whole town was there. Annie's father, Mr. Gayle, owned the bank and loaned Mr. Sledge some money and took a mortgage on his plantation, but times were hard and no one made a cotton crop for years and years and years, and Mr. Sledge couldn't pay anything on his mortgage and finally Mr. Gayle felt the bank couldn't carry him any longer and told him if he couldn't pay back the money he would have to take his plantation, and Mr. Sledge got into a fury when he heard that and went back home and got his gun, and as Mr. Gayle was coming out of the bank he shot him.

LEWIS. Was that how it was? What year was that?

FANNIE MAE. Oh goodness. I would say it was 1912. But don't hold me to that Lewis. Annie was at least 18. She saw the whole thing. *(Rain is heard again.)*

ALBERTA. Listen to the rain. It's just pouring now. *(There is lightning.)* It's lightning. *(There is thunder.)* It's thundering.

FANNIE MAE. *(Crosses to stage right door.)* It's supposed to rain all day and all night.

LEWIS. *(Crosses back to sit in his chair.)* I'll sleep well tonight, thank God. I always sleep well when it rains.

FANNIE MAE. *(Leaning against the door frame.)* I never sleep the whole night through, rain or not. Before Sitter May, who was my best friend since girlhood, died and I couldn't sleep, I'd get out of bed, put on my clothes and go quietly out of the house so as not to wake Mama and Bubba, and cross the street to Sitter May's house, who didn't sleep any more than I did, and I'd rap on her window. I didn't have to say a word, just rap, because I knew she'd know who it was, and sure enough out she'd come tiptoeing so as not to wake the rest of her family, and we'd get in my car and ride around to see what was going on until we got sleepy. Now Sitter's dead and I don't like to ride by myself, so Bubba gave me a little portable radio for Christmas that I keep by my bed, and now when I can't sleep, I turn on the radio and listen to people talk.

LEWIS. What do they talk about?

FANNIE MAE. Politics mostly. They holler and yell at each other. *(She looks over at Annie. She crosses to Annie as she remembers.)* Annie and I were both bridesmaids at Laura Ewing's wedding. Do you remember that Annie? Do you remember Laura Ewing's wedding? *(Sits next to Annie.)* Lo Griswold got her feelings hurt because she wasn't asked to be a bridesmaid. I wore a pink dress. Mama made it for me. What color was your dress, Annie? *(Annie doesn't answer or respond.)* I think it was blue. Was your dress blue, Annie? *(Again no response from Annie.)*

LEWIS. Where is Laura Ewing now? Is she alive?

FANNIE MAE. Yes, I'll say she's alive. She's a great-grandmother. *(To Annie.)* Did you know that, Annie? Laura Ewing is a great-grandmother? She lives in Dallas. She's had three husbands. One died and she divorced the other. She says with her third husband she has found happiness at last. *(Clarabelle crosses with towels from up right. She goes into the bathroom.)*

CLARABELLE. *(To Annie.)* Who brought Miss Annie Gayle in here?

FANNIE MAE. I did. I told her Alberta Thornton was here and she wanted to come and say hello. *(Clarabelle goes to the linen closet.)*

CLARABELLE. Did she say hello?

FANNIE MAE. Not yet.

CLARABELLE. *(At the linen closet.)* And she's not going to. She's been here three weeks and she ain't said a word yet.

LEWIS. She must have said something if she asked to come out here.

CLARABELLE. *(Coming down the stairs.)* Did she ask to come out here?

FANNIE MAE. No. She didn't ask. I told her Alberta Thornton was here and I bet she'd want to see her, and I took her by the arm and brought her out. *(The phone rings. Miss Pearl answers. Clarabelle sits in the stage right chair near the door.)*

MISS PEARL. Harrison Manor. Yes. Oh, yes. Well, that's all right. I understand. No. Yes. She has her clothes on. Yes. Thank you. *(She hangs up and crosses to Alberta.)* Miss Alberta, that was your cousin Douglas Jackson. He's going to be a little delayed. Some business has come up. *(Miss Pearl stands near the door.)*

ALBERTA. *(Gets up and marches toward her room.)* I know all about his business. Monkey business. Everybody in town knows about him. *(Turns from upstairs.)* Houston, too, now, because everybody I'd meet in Houston I'd tell about him. *(Walks away again and comes back.)* Don't ever hire him for your lawyer, because he'll steal you blind. *(At the top of the stairs.)* He wound up with Little Harry's farm and now he's bound and determined to get my duplex. Well, he'll never get it, because it's in my name. My duplex is in West University which is now a very expensive part of Houston. One day a man came to my door and knocked and I went to the door and he said, are you interested in selling your duplex? I can offer you a hundred thousand dollars cash, and I said, no, I'm not interested, and he left me his card in case I ever changed my mind. And the lady next door told me later that the same man had paid her a hundred and twenty-five thousand dollars, and she said he was just paying that for the land since he was going to tear the house down and put up a new house like they do in California.

LEWIS. They tore my house down you know. The Baptist Church tore it right down in front of my eyes. There's a parking lot there now.

FANNIE MAE. I don't think it was your house, Lewis. I think it was Gilbert Cunningham's house and when he died he left to the Baptist Church everything he had, including the house you rented.

LEWIS. I understand that, but Mama and I lived in that house over forty years. Everybody referred to it as our house. I paid my rent on time. Every time I brought my rent to Gilbert Cunningham he said I wish all my tenants were as dependable as you. If he had lived he would never let the Baptists tear my house down.

FANNIE MAE. I expect not.

LEWIS. *(Gets up and goes to Fannie Mae.)* I went to the Baptist Church regular as clock work every Sunday, but the day they tore my house down I vowed never to go again and I never have and I never will. *(Lewis exits. A pause. Clarabelle sits again. Miss Pearl sits at her desk.)*

ALBERTA. *(Standing at the middle of the stairs.)* I was certainly disappointed in Hollywood, Grauman's Chinese Theatre is there, but it's so tacky looking now and they have the footprints of stars on the sidewalk, but none I cared about. Where is Richard Barthelmes and Lila Lee and Lillian Gish and Mae Murray and Pola Negri and Bebe Daniels and Ben Lyons? I asked a man who looked like he knew everything. Who are they? he asked. Are they movie stars? Are they movie stars? I said, they certainly are. Well, their names are around here someplace then, he said, but I couldn't find those names anywhere. Mae Murray, they said, had bee stung lips and Richard Barthelmes was bowlegged, but he was awfully good looking. *(Annie calls out.)*

ANNIE. I want to go home. I want to go home.

FANNIE MAE. Why, she's talking, bless her heart. *(Clarabelle and Miss Pearl come over.)*

ANNIE. I want to go home. I want to go home.

CLARABELLE. I better take her back to her room. *(She leads her up the stairs and out upstage right. Annie struggles with Clarabelle. Pause. Alberta sits on the stairs watching them exit. Miss Pearl stands at the ramp and then sits at her desk.)*

FANNIE MAE. She has no home, you know. Her father was killed all those years ago, her mother's been dead at least twenty years. They brought her back here to be near her brother, I suspect, but he died last year, and his wife is in a retirement home now herself in Houston, a very expensive one, I hear. Of course, she has cousins, at least two that I know are living here.

MISS PEARL. She has a son somewhere in West Texas. He sent a check to keep her here.

ALBERTA. I have a home, I'm happy to say. It's a duplex in Houston, in West University, near Rice University. West University is very desirable. A man came to my door and wanted to buy my duplex. He had a hundred thousand dollars in cash. When I die I don't know where I'll be buried. The Thornton lot is all taken up. Rowena got the last space. My daddy is there, and my grandfather and grandmother and all my aunts. But there is no room for me there now at all. I'm the last of the Thorntons, you know, at least the last with the Thornton name, and I should certainly be buried with them. My mama is buried there next to my daddy, and she wasn't a Thornton, of course, but married to one. I said to Little Harry, if there's no longer room for me in the Thornton lot, I want to be buried as close to them as you can get me. Well, we'll see what we can arrange when the time comes, he said. I worry about it, you know, as he is very unreliable, has been all his life. Says one thing and does another. That's why I'll never let him get his hands on my duplex. Never in this world. Never. *(A pause. Lewis enters, crosses to his chair and sits.)* Do you all remember Punkin Armstrong? She was a sight that girl. Loved to drink. Got drunk at a dance one night and stood in the middle of the floor and yelled, I'm a Croom Armstrong aristocrat!

LEWIS. Where is Miss Punkin now?

ALBERTA. She's dead. She died after my sister Gloria, but before my sister Rowena. Rowena just played out. Don't leave me alone, Rowena, I said, please don't leave me alone. I'm tired honey, she said, I'm so tired and she turned over on her side and closed her eyes and I thought she was asleep. Little Harry came in then and he said, she's dead, Alberta, but I thought to myself you have been drinking again. But he was right because when I brought her supper I tried to wake her to eat it, I couldn't wake her. She was dead.

LEWIS. My God, everybody I know is dead. My mama, my sister, Edith, my little brother.

ALBERTA. When Rudolph Valentino died the whole nation went into mourning — *(Getting up and crossing to sit next to Fannie Mae on the couch.)* — and for the longest time every year after his death, they say, on the anniversary of his death a mysterious woman dressed all in black, her face covered by a black veil, visited his tomb. No one ever saw her face, but some say it was Pola Negri who threw herself on his coffin, sobbing, during the funeral. Do you think she was the mysterious lady in black?

FANNIE MAE. Are you asking me?

ALBERTA. Yes, ma'am.

FANNIE MAE. I wouldn't know, honey. It's the first time I've heard about it. What pictures was Pola Negri in? I can't remember

34

a single one.

ALBERTA. I can't either. I used to know them all. Rudolph Valentino was in *The Sheik*.

FANNIE MAE. Yes, I saw that. Did you see that, Lewis?

LEWIS. No, ma'am. I don't go to the picture show a whole lot. *(Gets up and crosses to stage left window.)* I guess I could count on my fingers the times I went to the picture show. *(Lewis looks out the window.)*

ALBERTA. I don't think it was Pola Negri, because she was living in San Antonio, Texas, after she left Hollywood, and Ludie Gordon moved to San Antonio after she got married and saw her twice there, and she said she was very heavy and if somebody hadn't pointed her out and told her who she was, she wouldn't have recognized her at all. *(He turns and faces them as he leans against the window.)*

LEWIS. The rain has stopped.

FANNIE MAE. Not for long. It's supposed to rain all day and all night. *(Alberta begins to sing.)* How does the rest of that song go, Alberta? *(Alberta sings a song of the period, such as "I Get the Blues When It Rains."* Fannie Mae joins in singing. Fannie Mae and Lewis clap.)* You have a sweet voice, honey. I had a pleasant voice at one time, you know. I sang in the choir at the Methodist Church. But I quit. Miss Anges Treat sang so loud she drowned everybody else out. I sang a solo once.

LEWIS. Sing it for us now.

FANNIE MAE. Oh no, Lewis. Heavens.

LEWIS. Come on, sing it.

FANNIE MAE. Well, all right. *(She sings a song of the period, such as "Beulah Land."* The front doorbell rings. Miss Pearl moves to open the door. Ora Sue comes back in with her grandmother in the wheelchair.)* ⟶ enter ⟶ left

MISS PEARL. Back so soon? I thought you were going to spend the day.

MRS. RUBY BLAIR. Another time. ⟶ going to center

ORA SUE. She ate something she said disagreed with her, and she said she needed to lie down. Mama said, well lie down here, but she said, no, she was used to her bed here and wanted to come

---

* See Special Note on Songs and Recordings on copyright page.

back. *(Clarabelle enters from upstage right and goes to the stairs.)*

MRS. RUBY BLAIR. My daughter loves cats. She's got six cats. There's a cat in every bed in her house. I don't want to lie down with cats.

ORA SUE. Well, just push them off the bed, Grandma.

MRS. RUBY BLAIR. What good does that do? They just hop right back up and I said to her mama, you're going to have to one day choose between me and the cats. Well, don't push it, she said, I might choose the cats.

ORA SUE. She was just joking, Grandma. *(Clarabelle comes down the stairs.)*

FANNIE MAE. Has Annie quieted down?

CLARABELLE. Yes. She's quiet.

MRS. RUBY BLAIR. I never could stand cats you know. That's why she has so many, she says, because I'd never let her have one growing up. Well, you had dogs, I said, and a horse and chickens and a billy goat and a nanny goat.

LEWIS. *(Moving toward his chair.)* Did you have all those animals here in town?

MRS. RUBY BLAIR. No, we lived out in the country. My husband was a rice farmer. When he retired we moved in here together. He fell over dead right here in this room.

CLARABELLE. He sure did. Right in front of me.

MRS. RUBY BLAIR. Every time I come through here I think about it.

ORA SUE. Come on, Grandmother.

MRS. RUBY BLAIR. Come on where?

ORA SUE. To your room. I have to take you to your room. I have pep squad practice. *(Clarabelle wheels her up the ramp. Ora Sue goes up the stairs and then resumes pushing the wheelchair offstage.)*

FANNIE MAE. Mama and I went to the Baptist Church for some reason or other one Sunday and in front of the church auditorium they had in big lettering: "One Lord, One Faith, One Baptism."

MISS PEARL. What does that mean? *(Miss Pearl crosses and waters the plants above and behind the couch.)*

FANNIE MAE. It means they believe in total immersion. We only sprinkle your head in the Methodist Church. *(Clarabelle re-enters and sits in her seat near the stage right door.)*

LEWIS. I remember like yesterday the day I was baptized. They took a bunch of us down to the river. I was the third, I remember. The preacher grabbed me and stuck my whole head under the water. What is your religion, Miss Alberta?

ALBERTA. I don't remember.

FANNIE MAE. I think you are Episcopalian, honey. What church are you affiliated with, Miss Pearl?

MISS PEARL. I was raised a Lutheran.

FANNIE MAE. We have a lovely Lutheran Church here.

MISS PEARL. Yes, Ma'am, I know, but I'm on duty here every Sunday it seems like.

FANNIE MAE. Clarabelle, what's your affiliation?

CLARABELLE. I'm a member of the Mother Zion Baptist Church.

lid they baptize you? In the river here?

No out in the country. In Peach Creek. I'd be
ed in the river here.

Why?

Because there are snakes there. Water moccasins,
le snakes, coral snakes. The river is alive with
goes back to her desk.)

any the day I was baptized. Used to be alligators
l gone. I haven't seen an alligator in I don't know
kson, 63, comes in the door and crosses to center stage.)
ernoon everybody.

fternoon.

Hello, Douglas.

s, you're looking well.

rning and meeting Miss Pearl in front of the ramp.)
'm sorry I was detained, Miss Pearl. I hope you
ienced.

That's all right. We're all having a good time

e you living here now, Miss Fannie Mae?

(Gets up.) No, I just brought some medicine for
l and Annie Gayle Long. She's living here now.

ss Annie Gayle Long?

Yes.

that right?

FANNIE MAE. She was in the A-S-Y-L-U-M, you know, for a number of years.

DOUGLAS. Yes, I remember.

FANNIE MAE. Douglas what church is Alberta affiliated with? She says she can't remember.

DOUGLAS. Episcopalian. All our family are Episcopalians.

FANNIE MAE. I thought so.

DOUGLAS. Well, Alberta, I have a present for you. *(He sits next to her on the couch and hands her a 9x12 envelope.)* Harry asked me to give you this. Why don't we go back in your room, so we can get a little visit in? *(Alberta doesn't answer him. She gets up and goes to stage left chair and sits, envelope in hands.)* Harry is out in the car. He'd like to come in and say hello to you. Shall I ask him in? *(No answer from Alberta. He gets up and works his way over to her.)* Harry and I have been working awful hard, you know, getting your affairs straightened out in Houston so you can stay here as long as you need to with peace of mind. He's a good boy, Alberta. He's made some mistakes admittedly but who hasn't? I've made mistakes, God knows. So let's all forgive and forget. After all, we're all Thorntons.

ALBERTA. You don't have the Thornton name and he doesn't have the Thornton name. I'm the last with the Thornton name.

DOUGLAS. I understand that, but we have the Thornton blood. We're still all Thorntons, the last of the Thorntons.

ALBERTA. That's not exactly true. We have a Thornton cousin in California and one in New York. Even though they don't have the name, they're Thorntons as much as you are.

DOUGLAS. Granted. You're looking well, Alberta, rested. *(To the others as he walks back toward Fannie Mae.)* When Alberta's mother died — how old were you when your mother died?

ALBERTA. Eight.

DOUGLAS. My mother, who was a widow, because my daddy died with the flu just a few weeks before her mother died — Did your mother die with the flu too, Alberta? I've forgotten.

ALBERTA. No, a broken heart.

DOUGLAS. Well, maybe so, but I bet it was the flu.

ALBERTA. It wasn't the flu, it was a broken heart, because of my —

DOUGLAS. *(Interrupting as he stands between the couch and*

Lewis' chair.) All right, if you say so. Anyway, the point of my story is that my mother had two boys but no girls and brought Alberta to our home and raised her, like she was her own daughter. I remember so the day Mama woke me up and said, son, I have a surprise for you. Your cousin Alberta's mother died and she's going to live with us. I want you to treat her like a sister and make her feel welcome. We were poor and didn't have much, but what we had we always shared with Alberta. Isn't that right, Alberta? *(Alberta doesn't answer.)*

LEWIS. I'd forgotten you had a brother. What happened to your brother?

DOUGLAS. He's dead. Died a long time ago. He didn't want to be buried back here. He's buried in Galveston. Alberta? *(Pause.)* If you've no objection I'm going to bring your nephew Harry in so he can say hello to you. He's come all the way from Houston to give you those pictures because he knew how much you wanted them. *(Pause.)* Alberta. *(Alberta doesn't answer. Miss Pearl waters plants behind her desk. Douglas leaves. Alberta opens the envelope. There are small pictures of her mother, Rowena and Gloria, Gloria's first husband, and 8x10's of Barbara La Marr and Rudolph Valentino. She takes the small pictures out. She gasps and rushes over to sit on the couch next to Fannie Mae.)*

ALBERTA. This is my mother.

FANNIE MAE. She's lovely. How old was she then, honey?

ALBERTA. I don't know. *(She shows Gloria's picture next.)* And this is my sister, Gloria. I know how old she was when this picture was taken. She was nineteen. And this is Rowena.

FANNIE MAE. Oh, yes. *(Alberta takes out a man's picture.)*

ALBERTA. And this is Gloria's husband that killed himself on their honeymoon. Gloria kept it all these years and just before she died she asked Rowena to bring her the picture, which she kept in her bureau drawer.

FANNIE MAE. What was his name, honey?

ALBERTA. Who?

FANNIE MAE. Gloria's first husband.

ALBERTA. William.

FANNIE MAE. William what?

ALBERTA. Chamberlain. From Mississippi. West Point,

Mississippi. He was a cotton buyer in Houston. He had bought this pistol so she could protect herself in Houston when he was away at work, and she said she went to turn off the gas stove for the night and he laughed and said, Gloria, if I thought you didn't love me I'd kill myself, and pulled the trigger and shot himself.

FANNIE MAE. Didn't he know the pistol was loaded?

ALBERTA. I reckon not. Anyway, Gloria was holding his picture in her hand when she died. I asked Rowena if I could have it, and Rowena said no at first as she thought his picture should be buried with Gloria, but then she changed her mind and said I could keep it. *(Harry, 35, and Douglas come in the door. Alberta puts the photos back in the envelope, crosses and sits in her stage left chair.)*

DOUGLAS. Harry, do you remember all these good people? This is Miss Fannie Mae Gossett. *(Harry comes over.)*

FANNIE MAE. *(Standing at the couch.)* How do you do? *(They shake hands.)*

HARRY. Fine, thank you. How do you do?

FANNIE MAE. I remember you as a little boy, and I knew your mama too, and your aunts and your great-aunts, and your grandparents, and your great-grandparents.

HARRY. Yes, ma'am.

DOUGLAS. And this is Mr. Lewis Reavis. *(Harry goes to him. They shake hands.)*

LEWIS. Howdy. I used to shoot pool in your granddaddy's pool hall. Mr. Albert Thornton. He was a real gentlemen. You never would have known he ran a pool hall.

DOUGLAS. *(Pointing to Clarabelle and Miss Pearl, both standing stage right.)* And these ladies both work here.

MISS PEARL. I'm Pearl and this is Clarabelle.

HARRY. How do you do.

MISS PEARL. Alberta was a little naughty earlier, but she's been real sweet the last hour. We are so proud of her.

LEWIS. Are you the one they took to Hollywood?

HARRY. Yessir. A long time ago.

CLARABELLE. Why did they take you to Hollywood?

HARRY. I had a screen test for a movie they were doing.

DOUGLAS. *(Standing next to the stairs.)* The Yearling. Did you ever hear of it?

CLARABELLE. No sir, I sure didn't.

DOUGLAS. Well, we almost had a movie star in our family. *(Harry laughs loudly.)*

MISS PEARL. Harry, didn't I see your picture in the *Houston Chronicle* not too long ago? Something about getting married by a computer?

HARRY. *(Center stage.)* Yes, ma'am. I'm afraid so.

MISS PEARL. It had a funny name. What name did they call it?

HARRY. Maritonics.

MISS PEARL. Maritonics.

HARRY. Yes, ma'am.

MISS PEARL. They had your picture in the paper. It was a real good likeness.

HARRY. Thank you.

CLARABELLE. How do you get married by a computer?

HARRY. Well … It's hard to explain. I wouldn't recommend it. *(Harry laughs loudly.)*

ALBERTA. You already have a wife in Mississippi and two lovely children.

HARRY. *(He crosses to the stage left.)* I don't have a wife in Mississippi. She's married to someone else now, Alberta. *(Harry is laughing. He jokingly mimics choking Alberta as he walks up behind her.)*

ALBERTA. Well, you did have.

DOUGLAS. *(Moving downstage.)* Let's change the subject, Alberta. That's all past history.

ALBERTA. I loved those children. It just broke my heart when she took them with her back to Mississippi.

DOUGLAS. *(Moving towards Alberta.)* That's all done, Alberta.

ALBERTA. That's all well and good for you to say. You never knew those children.

DOUGLAS. I certainly knew them, Alberta.

ALBERTA. But you never loved them like I loved them.

DOUGLAS. *(He goes to the magazine rack.)* Why don't we change the subject, Alberta?

HARRY. *(Kneeling next to Alberta.)* Are these the pictures you wanted from the duplex, Alberta?

ALBERTA. Yes, but you didn't have to bring them. I'm going

back, you know. Tomorrow or the next day. I've gotten over my nervousness. *(Douglas approaches her on the other side.)*

DOUGLAS. Now, Alberta, you know you can't go back. Be sensible.

ALBERTA. I certainly can go back. I left because I was nervous and I'm not nervous anymore.

DOUGLAS. You can't go back, Alberta. This is your home now.

ALBERTA. It's not my home. I have a duplex in Houston, and let's get this straight. You're never gonna get your hands on it. Never. You got his farm. *(Harry moves to the aquarium.)* Doesn't that satisfy you? You want everything? His farm, my duplex.

DOUGLAS. It wasn't just your duplex, Alberta. Part of it belonged to his mama, and Rowena.

ALBERTA. But it was to be mine, Rowena said, as long as —

DOUGLAS. *(Interrupting.)* It was practical for you to live there then, but it's no longer practical for you to live there now. You know that. You remember we had to go to court and let the judge decide what was in the best interest of all the parties, and he decided the best interest was to sell the duplex and use the money to bring you here and —

ALBERTA. *(Interrupting.)* I could have sold the duplex. A man came to my door and offered me a hundred thousand dollars in cash, but I said no. *(A pause.)* Is the duplex sold? Is that what you're trying to tell me?

DOUGLAS. You know that.

ALBERTA. Did that man that came to me buy it?

DOUGLAS. No.

ALBERTA. Who bought it?

DOUGLAS. I did, Alberta. You know that. *(Harry comes back down to stage left of Alberta as Douglas goes and gets a magazine.)*

ALBERTA. Of course you did. I said to Rowena just before she died, I said, he'll end up with everything, wait and see. Harry's farm, our duplex. *(To Harry.)* How much did he pay for it? *(Pause.)* I was offered a hundred thousand dollars —

HARRY. *(Interrupting and kneeling.)* No, you weren't Alberta.

ALBERTA. I certainly was, by a man who wanted to tear it down like they're doing in California.

HARRY. You just imagined that, Alberta —

ALBERTA. I did not imagine it. *(A pause.)* What happened to the furniture?

HARRY. It's all been sold.

ALBERTA. Sold?

HARRY. Yes, I had a yard sale. Don't you remember? I told you we were going to, and I asked you what you wanted out of the duplex and you said all you wanted were the pictures in your bureau drawer, and these were all I saw in the bureau drawer.

ALBERTA. And what about Rowena's clothes and Gloria's clothes?

HARRY. I sold them in the yard sale. I asked you if you wanted any of them and you said no, don't you remember?

ALBERTA. No, I don't remember. How much did you get at the yard sale?

HARRY. I can't tell you exactly. It wasn't a whole lot, but it was something. You'll get half of everything. Don't worry. Douglas is overseeing that. *(Alberta leaves to her room with the envelope. Clarabelle gets up to block the down right door.)* She's upset. Maybe we better go see to her. *(Douglas puts a magazine back in the rack and crosses to Miss Pearl. Harry sits in Alberta's chair.)*

DOUGLAS. Leave her alone. She'll get over it. Miss Pearl, the court has appointed me as her guardian. I'll be sending you the check every month.

MISS PEARL. Thank you.

DOUGLAS. And if there is anything extra she needs just let me know and I'll see it's taken care of.

MISS PEARL. Thank you.

DOUGLAS. Well, I guess we'd better be on our way, Harry.

HARRY. Yessir. *(They start out. Alberta re-enters from her room now carrying the small photos. She stands at the top of the stairs.)*

ALBERTA. Douglas?

DOUGLAS. Yes, Alberta?

ALBERTA. Are you going to tear the duplex down and put up a new house like they say everybody is doing in California?

DOUGLAS. No, I've already sold it.

ALBERTA. Are they going to tear it down and put up another house like they say everybody is —

DOUGLAS. *(Interrupting.)* I don't know what their plans are.

(Douglas stands at center stage.) You know, Miss Fannie Mae, the Thorntons weren't always Episcopalians. We were originally Baptists. Colonel Thornton was a big Baptist when he first came here. He built the First Baptist Church and insisted on having a balcony in the church so his slaves could have a place they could sit and listen to the preacher. But my grandmother and grandfather allowed my Mama and her sisters to play cards and dance, and one night when my grandmother was out nursing the sick, the Baptists had a meeting and expelled mama and her sisters from the church for dancing and card playing, and Mama said when Grandmother heard that she was so furious she took them all over to the Episcopalians, who didn't object to dancing and card playing, and they all became Episcopalians. You remember hearing that don't you, Alberta? *(Alberta doesn't answer, but stares at him. Again he starts out.)* Nice to have seen you all.

HARRY. Nice to have met you. *(Alberta goes down the stairs and sits on the couch next to Fannie Mae.)*

MISS PEARL. Come back anytime. *(Douglas again pauses and looks around as he stops next to Miss Pearl.)*

DOUGLAS. My children were all born here.

MISS PEARL. Is that so.

DOUGLAS. This used to be a hospital, you know. A long time ago it was a private home here, and two doctors bought it and turned it into a hospital and it was that for many years and then it was torn down and replaced with this nursing home.

MISS PEARL. Yes, I heard that today.

DOUGLAS. Goodbye. *(He and Harry leave. Alberta looks at her pictures.)*

ALBERTA. I don't have a picture of the duplex. I wish I had asked Harry to take a picture of it. Well, it's too late now. *(She looks at Rudolph Valentino's picture.)* I've saved Rudolph Valentino's picture and Barbara La Marr's picture all these years. This is the costume Rudolph Valentino wore in *The Eagle*. Do you remember seeing him in that picture, Miss Fannie Mae?

FANNIE MAE. No, I don't. He was handsome, wasn't he?

ALBERTA. Yes, he was.

FANNIE MAE. How old was he when he died?

ALBERTA. Thirty-one.

FANNIE MAE. Thirty-one. Is it possible? *(A pause.)* I loved him in *The Sheik*. How does that song go? "The Sheik of Araby?" Do you remember?

ALBERTA. *(Singing.)*
"I'm the Sheik of Araby.
Your love belongs to me."

FANNIE MAE. Oh, yes. That's it.

ALBERTA. *(Continuing to sing.)*
"At night when you're asleep
Into your tent I'll creep.
The stars that shine above
Will light our way to love
You'll rule this world with me,
I'm the Sheik of Araby."

(A pause.)

FANNIE MAE. That brings back memories, I'll tell you.

MISS PEARL. Was that a talking picture?

FANNIE MAE. No, honey. That was back in the early twenties. It was a silent picture. They didn't have talking pictures in those days. *(A pause.)* Who played in *The Sheik* with him?

ALBERTA. I forget.

FANNIE MAE. I think it was somebody Ayres. I can't remember her first name.

ALBERTA. It wasn't Pola Negri. I know that.

FANNIE MAE. No, not Pola Negri.

ALBERTA. She was Polish, you know.

FANNIE MAE. Is that so? Did Rudolph Valentino autograph his picture for you?

ALBERTA. Yes, he did. *(She hands the picture to her.)*

FANNIE MAE. *(Reading.)* To Alberta Thornton, sincerely Rudolph Valentino. My. And did Barbara La Marr autograph hers, too?

ALBERTA. Yes, she did. *(Reading.)* To Alberta Thornton. Lest ye forget, Barbara La Marr.

FANNIE MAE. Lest ye forget?

ALBERTA. Yes. When she died they said she was too beautiful to live.

FANNIE MAE. My. Lest ye forget. *(Annie Gayle Long comes back in. When Alberta sees her she stands and then backtracks downstage. Upset, she crosses towards the aquarium and avoids looking at Annie.)* Well, look who is here. Come sit down, Annie. *(She does so.)* Lest ye forget. *(She shows Annie Valentino's picture.)* Do you know who that is? That's Rudolph Valentino. *(Annie doesn't answer. Alberta turns to Fannie Mae.)*

ALBERTA. *(Agitated.)* I wonder how much Douglas paid for the duplex and how much he sold it for? I bet he made a good profit. Well, it's no use crying over spilt milk. What's done is done.

FANNIE MAE. Alberta, sing "The Sheik of Araby" for Annie. You would like to hear her sing it, wouldn't you, Annie? *(Annie makes no response. Alberta stands behind her stage left chair, turning sometimes towards Fannie Mae.)*

ALBERTA. I should have never left Houston in the first place, but then I got nervous, and I should never have left our home here. I said to Rowena at the time, are you sure we're doing the right thing? What else can we do, Bebe? As long as we stick together, we'll be all right. Stick together. That was Rowena's answer to everything. Stick together. Rowena and Gloria, and me. But they left me alone in our duplex in West University. All alone. And I got nervous, and I … *(A pause.)* I was always afraid of being left alone. I said that to Rowena, just before she died. Please don't leave me alone. *(She looks at her mother's picture.)* I don't remember very much about my mother. I remember crying when I was told she was dead, and I remember she always dressed the three of us, Rowena, Gloria, and me in white dresses, and I remember … *(A pause.)* Gloria wore black after her husband killed himself, and I said to Rowena, how long is she going to do that? and Rowena said, as long as it's proper, and she wore black for a year and I remember the day she stopped wearing it and a month later she began to go again with Harry Vaughn. *(A pause. She crosses toward Fannie Mae.)* I remember I had two beaux. Both handsome boys.

FANNIE MAE. Who were they, honey?

ALBERTA. One was James Lane, everybody called him Skinny. Skinny Lane. And the other was Wilson Davis.

FANNIE MAE. I remember Skinny Lane. He's dead, isn't he?

ALBERTA. Yes, he is.

FANNIE MAE. I don't remember Wilson Davis.

46

ALBERTA. He wasn't from here. He came in with an oil crew. Only stayed for six months. I don't know where he is now.

FANNIE MAE. Alberta, sing "The Sheik of Araby" for Annie. I think she'd enjoy it wouldn't you, Annie?

ALBERTA. *(Starting to sing.)* "I'm the Sheik of Araby." *(A pause.)* I forget the rest. *(Upset, she crosses and goes up the stairs toward her room. She stops and comes back. The first line is from the top of the ramp and she slowly works her way down to the middle of the ramp. She occasionally looks at the family photos in her hands.)* You know I have a duplex in West University, a very desirable part of Houston. I was offered a hundred thousand dollars for it recently but I turned it down, because that's where I lived with my sisters. We were known as the Thornton girls. And we always stuck together. Like Rowena said, they can't ever separate us. They've tried. When my mama died, our aunts, good women they were too, separated us. My Aunt Inez took Gloria, my Aunt Loula took Rowena, and Aunt Gert took me, but then Rowena got divorced, and Gloria became a widow and got divorced and we all came together and … *(A pause. She faces front.)* If only I hadn't gotten nervous, but I heard what I thought were slaves but they turned out to be hippies. And Rowena and Gloria were dead then. And I'm the last of the Thorntons. *(The lights fade a bit. A piano outlines a hauntingly slow variation of "The Sheik of Araby." Alberta looks up from her photographs and slowly mouths the words "Your love belongs to me …" She continues to sing/speak the words barely audible, if at all, of the song as the lights slowly dim leaving slight highlights on each character. They sit in silence. Alberta finishes her song with "into your tent I'll creep." She glances at her photos for a moment then silently stares out as the lights fade.)*

End of Play

PROPERTY LIST

Two small brown paper bags (FANNIE MAE)
Newspaper (LEWIS)
Towels (CLARABELLE)
Pitcher of water (MISS PEARL)
9x12 envelope containing small and 8x10 photos (DOUGLAS)
Magazine (DOUGLAS)

SOUND EFFECTS

Piano variation of "The Sheik of Araby"
Thunder
Torrential rain
Intercom buzzing
Telephone rings
Doorbell rings

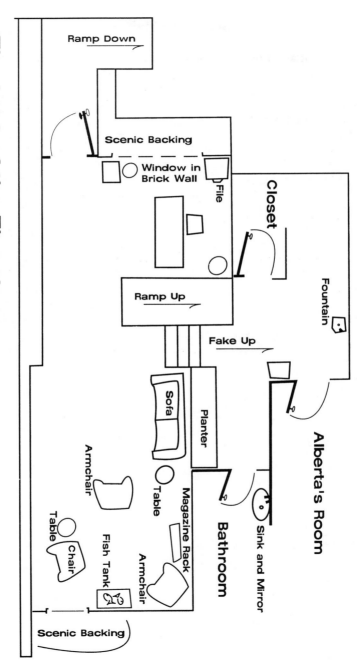

The Last of the Thorntons
Set Design by Christine Jones

Ramp Down

Scenic Backing

Window in Brick Wall

File

Closet

Fountain

Ramp Up

Fake Up

Alberta's Room

Sofa

Planter

Armchair

Table

Magazine Rack

Bathroom

Sink and Mirror

Table

Chair

Fish Tank

Armchair

Scenic Backing

NEW PLAYS

★ **AS BEES IN HONEY DROWN by Douglas Carter Beane.** Winner of the John Gassner Playwriting Award. A hot young novelist finds the subject of his new screenplay in a New York socialite who leads him into the world of *Auntie Mame* and *Breakfast at Tiffany's*, before she takes him for a ride. "A delicious soufflé of a satire ... [an] extremely entertaining fable for an age that always chooses image over substance." —*The NY Times* "... A witty assessment of one of the most active and relentless industries in a consumer society ... the creation of 'hot' young things, which the media have learned to mass produce with efficiency and zeal." —*The NY Daily News* [3M, 3W, flexible casting] ISBN: 0-8222-1651-5

★ **STUPID KIDS by John C. Russell.** In rapid, highly stylized scenes, the story follows four high-school students as they make their way from first through eighth period and beyond, struggling with the fears, frustrations, and longings peculiar to youth. "In STUPID KIDS ... playwright John C. Russell gets the opera of adolescence to a T ... The stylized teenspeak of STUPID KIDS ... suggests that Mr. Russell may have hidden a tape recorder under a desk in study hall somewhere and then scoured the tapes for good quotations ... it is the kids' insular, ceaselessly churning world, a pre-adult world of Doritos and libidos, that the playwright seeks to lay bare." —*The NY Times* "STUPID KIDS [is] a sharp-edged ... whoosh of teen angst and conformity anguish. It is also very funny." —*NY Newsday* [2M, 2W] ISBN: 0-8222-1698-1

★ **COLLECTED STORIES by Donald Margulies.** From Obie Award-winner Donald Margulies comes a provocative analysis of a student-teacher relationship that turns sour when the protégé becomes a rival. "With his fine ear for detail, Margulies creates an authentic, insular world, and he gives equal weight to the opposing viewpoints of two formidable characters." —*The LA Times* "This is probably Margulies' best play to date ..." —*The NY Post* "... always fluid and lively, the play is thick with ideas, like a stock-pot of good stew." —*The Village Voice* [2W] ISBN: 0-8222-1640-X

★ **FREEDOMLAND by Amy Freed.** An overdue showdown between a son and his father sets off fireworks that illuminate the neurosis, rage and anxiety of one family – and of America at the turn of the millennium. "FREEDOMLAND's more obvious links are to *Buried Child* and *Bosoms and Neglect*. Freed, like Guare, is an inspired wordsmith with a gift for surreal touches in situations grounded in familiar and real territory." —*Curtain Up* [3M, 4W] ISBN: 0-8222-1719-8

★ **STOP KISS by Diana Son.** A poignant and funny play about the ways, both sudden and slow, that lives can change irrevocably. "There's so much that is vital and exciting about STOP KISS ... you want to embrace this young author and cheer her onto other works ... the writing on display here is funny and credible ... you also will be charmed by its heartfelt characters and up-to-the-minute humor." —*The NY Daily News* "... irresistibly exciting ... a sweet, sad, and enchantingly sincere play." —*The NY Times* [3M, 3W] ISBN: 0-8222-1731-7

★ **THREE DAYS OF RAIN by Richard Greenberg.** The sins of fathers and mothers make for a bittersweet elegy in this poignant and revealing drama. "... a work so perfectly judged it heralds the arrival of a major playwright ... Greenberg is extraordinary." —*The NY Daily News* "Greenberg's play is filled with graceful passages that are by turns melancholy, harrowing, and often, quite funny." —*Variety* [2M, 1W] ISBN: 0-8222-1676-0

★ **THE WEIR by Conor McPherson.** In a bar in rural Ireland, the local men swap spooky stories in an attempt to impress a young woman from Dublin who recently moved into a nearby "haunted" house. However, the tables are soon turned when she spins a yarn of her own. "You shed all sense of time at this beautiful and devious new play." —*The NY Times* "Sheer theatrical magic. I have rarely been so convinced that I have just seen a modern classic. Tremendous." —*The London Daily Telegraph* [4M, 1W] ISBN: 0-8222-1706-6

DRAMATISTS PLAY SERVICE, INC.
440 Park Avenue South, New York, NY 10016 212-683-8960 Fax 212-213-1539
postmaster@dramatists.com www.dramatists.com

NEW PLAYS

★ **CLOSER by Patrick Marber.** Winner of the 1998 Olivier Award for Best Play and the 1999 New York Drama Critics Circle Award for Best Foreign Play. Four lives intertwine over the course of four and a half years in this densely plotted, stinging look at modern love and betrayal. "CLOSER is a sad, savvy, often funny play that casts a steely, unblinking gaze at the world of relationships and lets you come to your own conclusions ... CLOSER does not merely hold your attention; it burrows into you." *–New York Magazine* "A powerful, darkly funny play about the cosmic collision between the sun of love and the comet of desire." *–Newsweek Magazine* [2M, 2W] ISBN: 0-8222-1722-8

★ **THE MOST FABULOUS STORY EVER TOLD by Paul Rudnick.** A stage manager, headset and prompt book at hand, brings the house lights to half, then dark, and cues the creation of the world. Throughout the play, she's in control of everything. In other words, she's either God, or she thinks she is. "Line by line, Mr. Rudnick may be the funniest writer for the stage in the United States today ... One-liners, epigrams, withering put-downs and flashing repartee: These are the candles that Mr. Rudnick lights instead of cursing the darkness ... a testament to the virtues of laughing ... and in laughter, there is something like the memory of Eden." *–The NY Times* "Funny it is ... consistently, rapaciously, deliriously ... easily the funniest play in town." *–Variety* [4M, 5W] ISBN: 0-8222-1720-1

★ **A DOLL'S HOUSE by Henrik Ibsen, adapted by Frank McGuinness.** Winner of the 1997 Tony Award for Best Revival. "New, raw, gut-twisting and gripping. Easily the hottest drama this season." *–USA Today* "Bold, brilliant and alive." *–The Wall Street Journal* "A thunderclap of an evening that takes your breath away." *–Time Magazine* [4M, 4W, 2 boys] ISBN: 0-8222-1636-1

★ **THE HERBAL BED by Peter Whelan.** The play is based on actual events which occurred in Stratford-upon-Avon in the summer of 1613, when William Shakespeare's elder daughter was publicly accused of having a sexual liaison with a married neighbor and family friend. "In his probing new play, THE HERBAL BED ... Peter Whelan muses about a sidelong event in the life of Shakespeare's family and creates a finely textured tapestry of love and lies in the early 17th-century Stratford." *–The NY Times* "It is a first rate drama with interesting moral issues of truth and expediency." *–The NY Post* [5M, 3W] ISBN: 0-8222-1675-2

★ **SNAKEBIT by David Marshall Grant.** A study of modern friendship when put to the test. "... a rather smart and absorbing evening of water-cooler theater, the intimate sort of Off-Broadway experience that has you picking apart the recognizable characters long after the curtain calls." *–The NY Times* "Off-Broadway keeps on presenting us with compelling reasons for going to the theater. The latest is SNAKEBIT, David Marshall Grant's smart new comic drama about being thirtysomething and losing one's way in life." *–The NY Daily News* [3M, 1W] ISBN: 0-8222-1724-4

★ **A QUESTION OF MERCY by David Rabe.** The Obie Award-winning playwright probes the sensitive and controversial issue of doctor-assisted suicide in the age of AIDS in this poignant drama. "There are many devastating ironies in Mr. Rabe's beautifully considered, piercingly clear-eyed work ..." *–The NY Times* "With unsettling candor and disturbing insight, the play arouses pity and understanding of a troubling subject ... Rabe's provocative tale is an affirmation of dignity that rings clear and true." *–Variety* [6M, 1W] ISBN: 0-8222-1643-8

★ **DIMLY PERCEIVED THREATS TO THE SYSTEM by Jon Klein.** Reality and fantasy overlap with hilarious results as this unforgettable family attempts to survive the nineties. "Here's a play whose point about fractured families goes to the heart, mind – and ears." *–The Washington Post* "... an end-of-the-millennium comedy about a family on the verge of a nervous breakdown ... Trenchant and hilarious ..." *–The Baltimore Sun* [2M, 4W] ISBN: 0-8222-1677-9

DRAMATISTS PLAY SERVICE, INC.
440 Park Avenue South, New York, NY 10016 212-683-8960 Fax 212-213-1539
postmaster@dramatists.com www.dramatists.com

NEW PLAYS

★ **HONOUR by Joanna Murray-Smith.** In a series of intense confrontations, a wife, husband, lover and daughter negotiate the forces of passion, history, responsibility and honour. "HONOUR makes for surprisingly interesting viewing. Tight, crackling dialogue (usually played out in punchy verbal duels) captures characters unable to deal with emotions ... Murray-Smith effectively places her characters in situations that strip away pretense." *—Variety* "... the play's virtues are strong: a distinctive theatrical voice, passionate concerns ... HONOUR might just capture a few honors of its own." *—Time Out Magazine* [1M, 3W] ISBN: 0-8222-1683-3

★ **MR. PETERS' CONNECTIONS by Arthur Miller.** Mr. Miller describes the protagonist as existing in a dream-like state when the mind is "freed to roam from real memories to conjectures, from trivialities to tragic insights, from terror of death to glorying in one's being alive." With this memory play, the Tony Award and Pulitzer Prize-winner reaffirms his stature as the world's foremost dramatist. "... a cross between Joycean stream-of-consciousness and Strindberg's dream plays, sweetened with a dose of William Saroyan's philosophical whimsy ... CONNECTIONS is most intriguing ..." *—The NY Times* [5M, 3W] ISBN: 0-8222-1687-6

★ **THE WAITING ROOM by Lisa Loomer.** Three women from different centuries meet in a doctor's waiting room in this dark comedy about the timeless quest for beauty – and its cost. "... THE WAITING ROOM ... is a bold, risky melange of conflicting elements that is ... terrifically moving ... There's no resisting the fierce emotional pull of the play." *—The NY Times* "... one of the high points of this year's Off-Broadway season ... THE WAITING ROOM is well worth a visit." *—Back Stage* [7M, 4W, flexible casting] ISBN: 0-8222-1594-2

★ **THE OLD SETTLER by John Henry Redwood.** A sweet-natured comedy about two church-going sisters in 1943 Harlem and the handsome young man who rents a room in their apartment. "For all of its decent sentiments, THE OLD SETTLER avoids sentimentality. It has the authenticity and lack of pretense of an Early American sampler." *—The NY Times* "We've had some fine plays Off-Broadway this season, and this is one of the best." *—The NY Post* [1M, 3W] ISBN: 0-8-222-1642-6

★ **LAST TRAIN TO NIBROC by Arlene Hutton.** In 1940 two young strangers share a seat on a train bound east only to find their paths will cross again. "All aboard. LAST TRAIN TO NIBROC is a sweetly told little chamber romance." *—Show Business* "... [a] gently charming little play, reminiscent of Thornton Wilder in its look at rustic Americans who are to be treasured for their simplicity and directness ..." *—Associated Press* "The old formula of boy wins girls, boy loses girl, boy wins girl still works ... [a] well-made play that perfectly captures a slice of small-town-life-gone-by." *—Back Stage* [1M, 1W] ISBN: 0-8222-1753-8

★ **OVER THE RIVER AND THROUGH THE WOODS by Joe DiPietro.** Nick sees both sets of his grandparents every Sunday for dinner. This is routine until he has to tell them that he's been offered a dream job in Seattle. The news doesn't sit so well. "A hilarious family comedy that is even funnier than his long running musical revue *I Love You, You're Perfect, Now Change.*" *—Back Stage* "Loaded with laughs every step of the way." *—Star-Ledger* [3M, 3W] ISBN: 0-8222-1712-0

★ **SIDE MAN by Warren Leight.** 1999 Tony Award winner. This is the story of a broken family and the decline of jazz as popular entertainment. "... a tender, deeply personal memory play about the turmoil in the family of a jazz musician as his career crumbles at the dawn of the age of rock-and-roll ..." *—The NY Times* "[SIDE MAN] is an elegy for two things – a lost world and a lost love. When the two notes sound together in harmony, it is moving and graceful ..." *—The NY Daily News* "An atmospheric memory play ... with crisp dialogue and clearly drawn characters ... reflects the passing of an era with persuasive insight ... The joy and despair of the musicians is skillfully illustrated." *—Variety* [5M, 3W] ISBN: 0-8222-1721-X

DRAMATISTS PLAY SERVICE, INC.
440 Park Avenue South, New York, NY 10016 212-683-8960 Fax 212-213-1539
postmaster@dramatists.com www.dramatists.com